Whitchurch Street Names

For the stalwarts of Whitchurch – a few mentioned here, but many others unsung. With their time and talents they made the town what it is.

Whitchurch Street Names

Geoff Hide

Ellingham Press

2011

Copyright © Geoff Hide 2011

All rights reserved. No part of this book may be reprinted or reproduced or utilised in any form or by any electronic, mechanical or other means, now known or hereafter invented, including photocopying and recording, or in any information storage or retrieval system, without the permission in writing from the author.

ISBN   978-0-9563079-9-6

Published by Ellingham Press
43 High Street, Much Wenlock, Shropshire TF13 6AD
www.ellinghampress.co.uk

Typeset by ISB Typesetting, Sheffield, UK

Cover Design by The Goosey Graphics Company

www.gooseygraphics.co.uk

Printed by Bridgnorth Print, Bridgnorth, UK

Contents

Foreword	vii
Preface and Acknowledgements	ix
Introduction	xi
Origins of Whitchurch Street Names	1

Foreword

Whitchurch is a small town in the rolling chalk downs of north Hampshire, set at the intersection of two old coaching routes and with the river Test running through.

When Geoff asked me to write a foreword for this book I was chuffed to bits and felt greatly privileged. I am a local lad, as were my father Victor (Jack) and grandfather Frederick. And now, with my wife Sandra, we are proud to call Whitchurch our home where three generations of our family live. I have always loved the town and its people and seldom had any thoughts of moving from here. Many of the streets named in this book are places which I love to walk and explore and of which I never tire. My background is in building, from apprentice bricklayer to building surveyor, so you will understand that buildings, and the roads, lanes and paths that lead to them, are of abiding interest to me.

I am delighted to see this book published. Geoff is well qualified with his considerable family connections here. He has spent many hours of research to produce such an accurate and informative account of the roads serving Whitchurch in days gone by and still in use today.

This book gives meaning to so many names we see day by day on our street signs in the town. The historical facts accompanying those names give us an insight into the past and the people who helped make Whitchurch what it is today. It is a must for those of you who, like me, long to learn more about the reasons names appeared and disappeared over the recent past in Whitchurch.

I believe you will find this book as fascinating as I do. Through it you will learn so much about the history of this town. Through it we will also ensure that future generations have a knowledge of the history of Whitchurch and its people.

Barry J Jackman
Mayor of Whitchurch

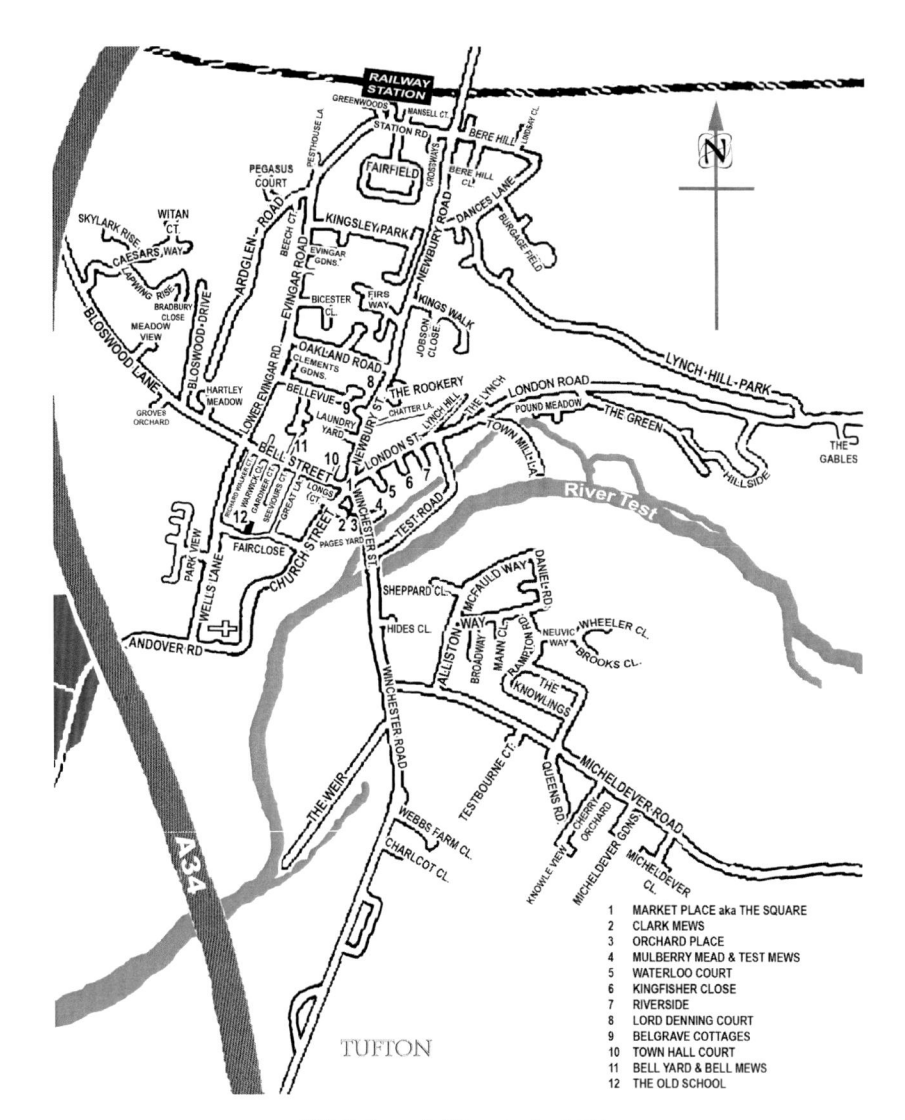

Whitchurch Streets in 2011

1 MARKET PLACE aka THE SQUARE
2 CLARK MEWS
3 ORCHARD PLACE
4 MULBERRY MEAD & TEST MEWS
5 WATERLOO COURT
6 KINGFISHER CLOSE
7 RIVERSIDE
8 LORD DENNING COURT
9 BELGRAVE COTTAGES
10 TOWN HALL COURT
11 BELL YARD & BELL MEWS
12 THE OLD SCHOOL

Preface and Acknowledgements

In 2009 the committee of Whitchurch History Society decided that a record should be compiled of the origin of names used for Whitchurch streets together with elements of their history. It was planned to involve members of the Society as well as others who were able to contribute such information. At first help was sought from the Town Clerk about the reasons for names suggested by the Town Council in recent building developments as well as those proposed by developers and submitted for approval. Mrs Burt also suggested that buildings and courts be included as they have been given names of local significance. Many residents of the town contributed and at the outset it became clear that this idea had been in the minds of several individuals and groups who had started bringing together similar information. This provided a valuable basis at the start of the project.

Such a compendium must be regarded as ongoing as the town will continue to expand and the density of dwellings increase by infilling so that more names will be required. Also, as this work is exposed to a wider audience, it is certain that errors and additional explanations will come to light.

I am grateful for generous help given by Alison Deveson and Martin Smith. The following also kindly contributed valuable information and discussion: Gillian Anderson, Peggy Baker, David Broad, Tom Brooks, Cathy Burt, Irene and Ken Clark, Michael Claxton, Beryl and Ron Clowes, Mary Collis, Ron Cook, Pat Cooper, Marion Cornford, David Culley, Tony Duddington, Julie and Richard Elston, Beryl and Ron Gammon, Myrtle Glendon, Jessie Golding, Hector Goldsack, Gerald Gregory, Frances Hide, Barry Jackman, Geoff Kelland, June Kent, Joan Lindsay, Geraldine Mouat, David Old, Ken Rampton, Jean and Neville Richards, Dorothy Ruffell, Pauline and Peter Rutter, Bill Sharpe, Beryl Smith, George Smith, Glenys Smith, Roy Smith, Barbara Steeden, Jean Treble, Sheila Vallence, Deirdre Walker, Gill Webb, Ruth Wigmore, Claire Wilson and Richard Wiltshire.

Whitchurch Street Names

Also consulted were Lloyd Stratton's *Whitchurch United: The History of a Football Club* (2004), documents given to the Society from the collection of Freda Jobson and the archive of Jim Chard, founder member of Whitchurch Local History Society, now Whitchurch History Society, which was generously donated by his daughter Maureen Llewellyn. The photographs, taken in the early 1900s, were prepared for publication by Hector Goldsack, who also kindly drew the map of Whitchurch streets in 2011. I thank Roy Smith for the use of his re-drawing of Laurence's 1730 map of Whitchurch.

Introduction

At the time of the Domesday Survey in 1086 Whitchurch was included in the Hundred of Evingar together with Freefolk, Hurstbourne Priors and Clere. The Hundred was enlarged in the thirteenth century to include Ecchinswell, Ashmansworth, East Woodhay and Newtown. Among earlier names for Whitchurch were Hwitan cyrice (tenth century), Witcerce (eleventh century) and Witcherche, Whitecherche (twelfth and thirteenth centuries). It is suggested that the name derives from a 'white church' likely to have been built with flints and hard chalk in *c.* AD 800, and this probably provided the focus for the first settlement.

The earliest references to street names are in a manuscript called the Winchester Cathedral Custumal which listed the possessions of Winchester Cathedral Priory in the thirteenth century. When Whitchurch was laid out as a new town in 1251 its streets were called *magnus vicus*, *Wodestret*, *Bynstret* and *Mulestret*. The second and fourth retained their names into the eighteenth century, being shown on the earliest extant map of Whitchurch, dated 1730, by Laurence (see inside back cover) as Wood Street and Mill Street, now Bell Street and London Street respectively. Wood Street was named after Blows Wood and Mill Street after the corn mill mentioned in the Domesday Survey, now called Town Mill.

Magnus vicus (great or high street) became Church Street and it was intended to be the main street of the medieval new town. However, *Bynstret* is more problematical. The only remaining medieval streets with which it could be identified are Newbury Street (Bearhill Street on the 1730 map) and Winchester Street (Duck Street). But it is possible that it referred to the whole length of the Newbury to Winchester road, considered as one street. Another theory, yet to be fully explored, is that the present Winchester Street is a relatively late route, and that the road from Winchester to Whitchurch originally led across the water meadows directly to the church so that the river would need to be forded only once. If this were so, then *Bynstret* would have been the original name of Newbury Street only.

But Whitchurch did not develop as a settlement round the church and by the time that the market and borough were established in the thirteenth century it had moved eastwards to the meeting of five roads. Early street names were derived from physical features of the settlement (Mill Street, Church Street, Knowle Lane, etc.). With the expansion of the town in the twentieth century, rather than using names which might have no local significance, the Town Council thought it appropriate to honour members of Whitchurch society who had contributed to its wellbeing, although also still including features of the town (e.g. Burgage Field, Caesars Way and Hillside).

The earliest forms of local government date from Anglo-Saxon times when Whitchurch was included in the Hundred of Evingar and hundredal courts administered justice and were responsible for the maintenance of roads. The Andover to Basingstoke road became a turnpike in 1754 and the Winchester to Newbury road in 1762, and tolls collected were used to keep the roads in good repair. By the nineteenth century groups of parishes were brought together and known as Unions to build workhouses, to house and find work for the poor as well as having responsibility for roads and bridges. Boards of Guardians were elected by local ratepayers and supervised these Unions.

However, towards the end of the nineteenth century rural poverty had declined, whereas road travel and public health were matters of importance and a Local Government Act of 1894 required the further grouping of parishes. Whitchurch Rural District Council was constituted in 1907 and comprised the parishes of Whitchurch, Overton, Laverstoke and Hurstbourne Priors. It was governed by elected councillors. Then in 1932, following a further Local Government Act of 1929, the individual Whitchurch and Kingsclere Rural District Councils were amalgamated as Kingsclere and Whitchurch Rural District Council. In 1974 and following a Royal Commission this council was abolished and responsibilities were transferred to the larger Basingstoke & Deane Borough Council to which the town sends elected councillors. The town's mayoralty was restored and Whitchurch now has a Town Council of elected councillors. All local roads are currently the responsibility of Hampshire County Council.

Origins of Whitchurch Street Names

Alliston Way Archibald Alliston was a civil servant who came as a surveyor with staff of the Bank of England's Dividend Preparation Office when they took up residence in Hurstbourne House (The Mansion) in August 1939 at the start of the Second World War. The staff soon moved to Overton to make way for the bank's Accounts Department which had office and domestic accommodation built in Hurstbourne Park as well as occupying several houses in the town. Staff stayed here until hostilities ceased in 1945. Archie then remained in Whitchurch to work for the Royal Army Pay Corps when the detachment continued use of these buildings and he became chairman of the Town Council in 1951. He supported the British Red Cross Society in Whitchurch and became a dealer in antiques from his shop in London Street.

Andover Road The continuation of Church Street beyond the church. The stretch of road passing Hurstbourne Park was earlier called Great Western Road and almost at the end of the park's brick perimeter wall is Bull's Gate, the boundary of Whitchurch parish.

Ardglen Road While this industrial estate was being developed in the 1980s, John Clarke, solicitor, consulted Companies House and chose the name Ardglen from a list of defunct companies. It had no local significance.

Beech Court Mature beech trees grew here before apartments were built.

Belgrave Cottages Four nineteenth-century dwellings to the rear of Belgrave House, a 3-storey mellow red brick house and the home of Dr Edward Burgess, physician and surgeon in the early twentieth century. Causeway House next door was the home of Dr Henry Hemsted (1837–1916), also a local surgeon and Medical Officer of Health at the Whitchurch Isolation Hospital on the Kingsclere Road. His father, Tobias Rustat Hemsted (1810–80), and son, Henry Rustat Hemsted (1869–1958), were also doctors living here.

Bell Street Originally called *Wodestret* in the thirteenth-century Winchester Cathedral Custumal, it became Wood Street and was named after nearby Blows Wood. This name continued in use until it was listed as Bell Street in the 1881 Census, no doubt from the Bell Inn which is known to have been a public house from about 1710. It has been suggested that the name was changed to Bell Street on the recommendation of James Thomas Bingham, JP (1839–1914), a prominent businessman in the town. (See **Bloswood Lane**.)

Bell Yard This area was known as **Veagles** in the thirteenth and fourteenth centuries from the family living here at the time. The building now called the Bell Inn was built for the manufacture of woollen cloth in the seventeenth century by the Brooke family who lived in Parsonage Farm (later The Vicarage and now Kings Lodge). After it had been washed and dyed the cloth was put out to dry on pole-like structures known as racks and the area of land extending up to where Oakland Road was called **Rack Close**. This name still appeared in deeds of the 1950s. More recently the thoroughfare led up to the Whitchurch brickworks, thought to have been in production between 1850 and 1900, and passed a smithy and motor engineering works run by Henry Sampson from the late 1890s for about 30 years. It was then called **Sampsons Yard**. Presumably its name was changed when Wood Street became Bell Street. Also **Bell Mews**.

Bellevue During the construction of houses in 1969, the area was known informally as Bell View as it was within sight of the Bell Inn, an ancient hostelry. However, the Council later confirmed the name with a different spelling.

Bere Hill (See **Newbury Street**.)

Bicester Close Samuel Bennett (1866–1933), a grocer from Bicester, Oxfordshire, came to Whitchurch in the early 1900s to lease Jesse Long's grocery shop in the Market Place so that Long could concentrate on his jam manufacturing business. Bennett became vice-chairman of Whitchurch Rural District Council and the first chairman of Whitchurch United Football Club in 1903, subsequently serving on the committee for more than 20 years. He and his family lived in accommodation above the shop and as the business prospered he built Bicester House on a plot north of the town centre after the First World War.

Origins of Whitchurch Street Names

Bell Street
The Plough Inn, now a private residence, was built in 1441 and became a beer-house in 1846. Beyond the windows of Duddington's hardware shop is the arched entrance to the coal-fired boiler of Long's jam factory.

Bloswood Lane A continuation of Wood Street (Bell Street) outside the medieval town as Blows Wood lay to the west of the lane. It was earlier known as Blowswood, Blosewood or Blowerswood Lane.

Bloswood Drive Building commenced in 1956 on what was known as Cinder Track that led past a hockey field on the corner with Bloswood Lane, later to become the Whitchurch bowling green. The track then passed allotment gardens and Marjorie Claxton's glasshouse nursery which started here in 1938 and continued until 1973. Further on was Mr Hunter's plantation that extended up to the London and South Western Railway line and supplied fruit to Jesse Long's jam manufacturing business. This plantation was later taken on by Peter Jones.

Bradbury Close Douglas Bradbury (1931–98), town councillor and mayor in 1988, was a founder member of the Twinning Association of Whitchurch with Neuvic, France. He bequeathed a considerable sum to this as well as to towards the purchase of a water meadow that was to become Millennium Meadow. His generosity to the Whitchurch surgery is commemorated as the Bradbury Room. (See **Neuvic Way**.)

Broadway David Edward Broad (1901–78) was born in Barton Stacey and came to Whitchurch from West Dean near Salisbury in

1938. He was employed by the Southern Railway with responsibility for the track several miles west of Whitchurch and beyond Hurstbourne. During the Second World War he joined the town's St John Ambulance Brigade and remained a member for several years, becoming proficient in teaching First Aid. Eddie was a town councillor in the 1950s with a special interest in footpaths and bridleways. As one of the important characteristics of Whitchurch is the well-established interconnecting network of footpaths and alleyways, it is due to him and his successors that these have been retained and are still widely used.

Brooks Close Thomas Brooks was born at Southfield Farm in Knowle Lane and apprenticed as an electrician at Thorneycroft in Basingstoke. After military service Tom was employed at AWRE Aldermaston for 34 years. He was elected a councillor in 1986 and for 17 years represented the town on the Basingstoke & Deane Borough Council.

Burgage Field The Priory of Winchester issued a charter for the establishment of a borough (town) of Whitchurch in 1248/9, and the 1251 Whitchurch Borough Rental held in Winchester Cathedral Library lists the tenants (burgesses) and the rents paid for their burgage plots. These were mostly narrow two-acre strips of land contained within the manor's open fields that could be used as gardens or for workshops, outbuildings and stables. The rent was collected by the reeve or bailiff, a position later called mayor, who was the Priory's representative in Whitchurch. Most burgage plots were still in existence in the 1830s and many were found on the north side of London Street. The current Burgage Field is situated on the site of burgage plots that had been created out of Lock Field, one of the three medieval open fields belonging to the parish.

Caesars Way In advance of building on this area north of Bloswood Lane and east of the Whitchurch bypass (and proposed to be called Fox (or Foxcote) Mead and Saxon Grove), the developers and Hampshire County Council funded archaeological investigations of crop marks on the site. Excavations and aerial and geophysical surveys in 1998 revealed a Romano-British cemetery containing five inhumations including a child aged about four years of age. These results were received enthusiastically by the Town Council and also by local people, and consequently AOC Archaeology and Berkshire Archaeological Services submitted a proposal to the County Council for funding a programme of research offering scope for the involvement of volunteers. Under the guidance of archaeologist Dr Roy Entwistle, more than 20 local people excavated in June and July 1999 and also assisted in the interpretation of features being uncovered. The findings included walled enclosures, quarry pits, human and animal bones, tiles and pottery. Occupation of the site was dated between 310 BC and AD 100. The earliest features were the burial of two neonatal infants and a Middle Iron Age storage pit containing the remains of two dogs. A further dig was proposed on the opposite side of the A34 bypass because preliminary observations suggested that it might yield Roman remains, but permission to investigate was not given by the landowner.

Charlcot Close/Farm Charlcot was a tithing of Evingar Hundred and in 1281 was owned by the Prior and Convent of St Swithin, but granted to their successors the Dean and Chapter in 1541. The name Charlcot probably derives from the Old English *ceorlacote* meaning cottages of villeins (ceorls). These were peasants or tenant farmers who were tied to an estate. In documents from at least 1597 it was Charlcote whereas the current name has been used from the 1780s.

Chatter Lane Several explanations have been proposed for the origin of this name, but none so far suggested stands up to scrutiny. From the 1730s and up to the 1960s it was known as Chatter Alley, Charter Alley or The Alley and gave access to a Friends (Quaker) meeting house and burial ground. Early in the twentieth century this footpath was also known as The Lynch which it joined near the chalk escarpment, and at this time it was informally called The Crot.

Cherry Orchard A name proposed by the developer because there were cherry trees in the garden of the house previously occupying the site.

Church Street As suggested earlier this could have been called *magnus vicus* (great or high street). The parish church, originally called All Saints and now All Hallows, was built on the site of what was one of the earliest churches in Hampshire and has surviving architectural features of the twelfth to the fifteenth centuries. It is thought that the town took its name from the 'white church', no doubt built of local flints and hard chalk, or even rendered and whitewashed, which must have existed here in AD 800. It was largely rebuilt and then given a spire in 1887/8 when an Anglo-Saxon gravestone dated to the mid ninth century was recovered from the wall of the tower. A short path that originally led down a slope from the church to the bend in Church Street, still distinguishable in the flint and brick retaining wall, was known locally as **Dudley Slip**. Legend has it that the Reverend William Mason Dudley, vicar of Whitchurch 1844–86, chased a misbehaving choirboy down the path and fell in mud…

Whitchurch Street Names

Church Street
This picture shows shops in the Market Place and in the distance the Kings Arms that was built in c. 1575 and became an inn in 1675. During the Civil War troops of King Charles I were billeted here in October 1644 before the second Battle of Newbury. The King stayed at Parsonage Farm, built in the 1600s and now called Kings Lodge, close by All Saints (All Hallows) Church.

Church Street
All Hallows Church is in the background with, on the left, the garden wall of The Lawn which was used by the Bank of England during the Second World War and was the home of Lord Denning 1963–2000. On the right is the garden wall of The Mount, a mid Victorian mansion set in three acres of land.

Origins of Whitchurch Street Names

Clark Mews Irene and Ken Clark came from Bournemouth in 1963 to manage the seed and coal merchants in Church Street owned by J R Wood and later by Corralls. Ken was a town councillor for 18 years and mayor from 1993 to 1995. He was secretary of the Whitchurch branch of the British Legion for 23 years and later chairman. In addition he was treasurer of the Whitchurch Scout Group for 15 years, and treasurer of the District Division of the Girl Guides. Irene was also a councillor for 10 years and mayor in 2001 and again in 2005. For 15 years she organized the British Legion Poppy Appeal and was herself a Guider, Brownie Guider and District Commissioner.

Clements Gardens The land comprised the garden of George (1912–79) and Emily Clements (1909–2003). George was a notable local builder.

Crossways The name of a house that stood diagonally across the south corner of Newbury Street and Station Road. This was the home of Edward Dance of Bere Hill Farm and was demolished for the development.

Dances Lane originally led past Portal's cricket ground to Bere Hill Farm which comprised 237 acres, part of which had been worked by Jonathan Dance (1836–1908) since the late 1870s and which the family bought from the Portal's Laverstoke Estate in 1921. His son Edward John (1869–1912) was born there and took on Wooldings Farm but came back to Bere Hill, which in turn was later worked by his sons Jonathan Eric Dance (1900–72) and Edward William Dance (1904–70). During the Second World War local schoolchildren were given an autumn holiday to help harvest potatoes here. (See **Crossways**, **Pesthouse Lane**.)

Daniel Road Bernard Daniel (1904–79), town councillor and mayor in 1978, was a shopkeeper with provision shops in Winchester Road and London Street. He was a founder member of the Twinning Association (see **Neuvic Way**) and a notable photographer.

Evingar Road As noted above, the Domesday Survey of 1086 placed Whitchurch in the Hundred of Evingar. The name is not associated with any settlement in the locality. (See **Pesthouse Lane**.)

Fairclose Fairs were held on a meadow and two old orchards to the north of Church Street and up to what became known as Wells Lane. These had been granted to Lord Russell in 1696 and four fairs were held annually from 1795; two were still held each year in June and in October in the 1800s. Before 1696 the area was known as White's Close and Old Garden.

Fairfield Originally part of the Portal's Laverstoke Estate, this area was later owned by Frederick Weeks who sold it to the Town Council. During the Second World War the southernmost part of the meadow was used as a camp, firstly for German prisoners of war who were later transferred to Kentucky, USA, and then for Italian prisoners who helped maintain the nearby railway line and also worked on local farms. At the end of the war German prisoners were again held here. The reason for the name is not known and in recent times it seems to have become plural.

Firsway Coniferous trees had been planted across this area when it was part of the Portal's Laverstoke Estate. Prefabricated homes, both two-storey sectional concrete houses and pairs of bungalows made of aluminium at the Bristol aircraft factory, were built after the Second World War. Mrs Olive Clarke, town councillor and husband of Col. J T P Clarke, solicitor, visited the new residents to gain their ideas on what the road should be called. Firsway was the one chosen by them and approved by the Town Council.

The Gables Built as the Union Workhouse in 1847/9 at a cost of £4,300 to provide accommodation for 120 inmates, it was enlarged in 1861 and again in 1900. It was used as a convalescent home for soldiers returning from the Second Boer War (1899–1902) and also from the First World War. Then it became a home for elderly folk until 1939 when the Bank of England took over the premises for their staff, and the residents were moved to Stockbridge. They returned in September 1945, but it soon became a home for children. After a few years it was again a home for elderly folk. Hampshire County Council sold the building in 1966 and it was converted into residences.

Gardner Court Lilian May Gardner (1897–1982), born in London where she started her nursing and midwifery training, was initially posted to Sutton Scotney and later to Somerset. She arrived in Whitchurch in 1932 and became a well-respected and familiar figure about the town, being driven to appointments by her husband Roy. Not only a district nurse, Nurse Gardner supervised the birth in Whitchurch of more than 940 babies during 26 years and on occasion was known to deal with six births in one day.

Great Lane Although the five main streets of the town are given names on the 1730 map of Whitchurch, Great Lane appears to be the only other prominent thoroughfare in the town but it is not given a name. A document dated 1708 relating to the Independent Chapel

Origins of Whitchurch Street Names

The Gables
This was built as the Union Workhouse in 1847/9, renamed The Gables in the early twentieth century and converted into private apartments in the 1960s.

(demolished in 1969), which stood on the eastern side about half way along between Wood (Bell) Street and Fairclose, requested a licence from the Bishop of Winchester for a 'House in Whitchurch for the worship of God fronting to a lane called Mans Lane'. In later documents it is also variously called 'Mans or Squires Lane' and on an 1839 map 'Great or Mans Lane'. In it was a group of thatched cottages known as Square (or Squires) Gardens or The Square which were occupied mostly by workers involved in the local silk industry. The cottages were destroyed when a fire took hold in the thatched roof on 28 May 1959; they were later demolished and residents moved to houses in Evingar Road.

The Green Town and village greens were commonly grass areas at the centre of settlements that were used for grazing or watering livestock from the common field. How this applied to Whitchurch is not known although the name does appear in 1841 Census returns. Certainly water was plentiful as more recently the area supported watercress beds. (See **Pound Meadow**.)

Greenwoods Charles (Charlie) Greenwood was manager of Davis Products' soap factory situated near to the Southern Railway station and producing Davex soap and soap flakes. During the Second World War the company manufactured glycerine for explosives. The factory closed in 1966. Nearby, at an earlier date, was John Kelland's chaff works where chaff that arrived by train was ground to make horse fodder. Much of this went to the Western Front in France during the First World War.

Groves Orchard Wilfred Groves (1913–89) came from Mansfield, Nottinghamshire to Whitchurch when he was 22 years old to work in the soap factory and was soon promoted to 'soap maker'. During the Second World War he joined the RAF, became a sergeant fitter and was Mentioned in Dispatches. Wilf returned to the soap factory after the war and when it closed became an electrician with Wiltshire & Rimmer, suppliers and repairers of radios and televisions in the Market Place. In retirement he remained fully occupied giving practical help to his many friends and neighbours – a true stalwart of Whitchurch.

Hartley Meadow had earlier been called Foster's Field and was purchased by J Long Ltd, jam manufacturers, in 1924 from Charles Rampton. A motor garage was built and called the Bell Engineering Works that was managed by Frank Stevens and serviced the company's vehicles as well as competing for outside work. Long's jam factory in Bell Street closed in 1950 and was later used by another jam maker, Crosbie's Pure Food Company Ltd. The houses and apartments in Hartley Meadow were built in the early 1990s and the name is assumed to come from another contemporary prominent jam manufacturer, although Hartley must have been among Long's competitors.

Hillside Part of the site was previously occupied by allotment gardens that sloped southwards down to The Green. The name for this area proposed by the developer did not meet with the approval of the first residents who then suggested the current name.

Hides Close James Hide (1866–1955), town councillor, trustee of the Town Hall for more than 30 years and silk manufacturer, bought the land next to The Elms where he lived from Sir Wyndham Portal in 1910 for a garden and tennis court that was used by many local players. After his death it was bought by his nephew Arthur who sold it in 1978.

Jobson Close James Jobson was an electrician and one of the first employees at the AWRE, Aldermaston. After the Second World War he installed an electrical generator working off the water wheel at the Silk Mill to power winding, warping and weaving machinery as well as lighting. Jim was a councillor on the Kingsclere & Whitchurch Rural District Council and instrumental in lobbying for the A34 bypass that was opened in 1976. His wife Freda (née Ford), previously a secretary at Long's jam factory of which her father was a director, was the local Conservative Party secretary and involved in the National Savings movement for 35 years. She was also a Guider and from 1929 a member of the British Red Cross Society in Whitchurch. During the Second World War Freda worked for the Bank of England in Hurstbourne Park.

Kingfisher Close As a new name for an old thoroughfare it celebrates the bird that nests in banks of the river Test nearby, and on which Ron and Rosemary Eastman made a study from their home at Town Mill. This culminated in their remarkable film *The Private Life of the Kingfisher* first shown on BBC Television in 1966. Three years later Rosemary published her book *The Kingfisher*. Ron and Rosemary were pioneers in producing natural history films that won worldwide acclaim.

Kings Walk Albert Sidney King (1918–89) was born and lived all his life in the cottage in London Street now called Kings Cottage. After working at the Laverstoke paper mill he volunteered for military service in 1939 but was soon invalided out. On his return to Whitchurch Bert became involved with sports and social clubs, but it was his work in keeping the streets of Whitchurch tidy that put him in the best position for gleaning news of events in the town. He was the local correspondent for the *Andover Advertiser*, *Hampshire Chronicle* and *Basingstoke Gazette*, and for 17 years contributed a column in the Parish Magazine. Bert's knowledge of townsfolk was used to advantage in arranging beaters for pheasant shoots for the farming community.

Kingsley Park The Reverend Charles Kingsley (1819–75), sometime vicar of Eversley, came to Whitchurch on a fishing holiday and stayed at the White Hart Hotel. Although he is chiefly known for his novel *The Water Babies*, first published in 1863, in an earlier book *Two Years Ago* (1857) details of Whitchurch are thinly disguised as 'Whitbury'. The name was first used in the Kingsley Temperance Hotel built at the corner of London Street and the Market Place on part of the site previously occupied by the Whitchurch post office and John Roe's brewery. This building now houses the Newbury Building Society and several offices.

Knowle View Jack and Edna Enright built a bungalow on the west side of Micheldever Road and called it The Knowle. Sometime later the name was modified and used for The Knowlings, a development on the opposite side of the road. The bungalow was demolished in 2004 and a group of houses built on the plot now called Knowle View. (See **Micheldever Road**.)

Whitchurch Street Names

Knowle Lane
This picture looks towards the junction with Winchester Road. This lane, now called Micheldever Road, was still unmade in 1917. Four houses on the right have flat roofs and it is thought that this was at the request of the Portal family, who lived in Berehill House, so that their guests travelling from Winchester could be seen by telescope before they arrived.

The Knowlings Proposed to be called The Crescent, Coronation Close, the dwellings were not built in time for the 1953 event. (See **Knowle View**, **Micheldever Road**.)

Lapwing Rise During archaeological excavations on an area north of Bloswood Lane in 1999 by members of the Whitchurch community (see **Caesars Way**), the town mayor Gill Nethercott observed lapwings and skylarks in the fields. Also **Skylark Rise**.

Laundry Yard Whitchurch Hand Laundry was started in the 1930s by Mr and Mrs Hodgson and subsequently run by Edward Piggott. Jesse Long's mineral waterworks, managed by William Lambden, was housed in a malt-house at the entrance to Laundry Yard but later moved to a new factory built behind the Bell Engineering Works in Bloswood Lane (see **Hartley Meadow**). Also in this area was a builder's yard belonging to Frederick Weeks (1867–1959), master builder and superintendent of the fire brigade, who provided a shed for the local manual fire engine from 1897 to 1914.

Lindsay Close Ian Lindsay (1928–2005), born in Catford, southeast London, was the son of Arthur Lindsay who had charge of the power house at Portal's paper mill. He followed his father into the electrical industry and after service in the RAF as an electronics instructor he worked at the Logie Baird factory in Sydenham. Ian later joined Wiltshire & Rimmer, radio and television retailers and repairers, in the Market Place as an engineer. When this shop closed in 1962 he opened his own in London Street where for 12 years he sold and repaired electrical equipment, invariably charging much less than he could. Ian was a town councillor and had a wide range of interests including music and humour. Appropriately Lindsay Close adjoins his former home in Bere Hill.

London Street Originally this was called *Mulestret* (Mill Street) as giving access to Town Mill, later called Lloyd's Mill. By the 1870s it was called London Street and at present becomes London Road at the bend in the road about 100m from the access to Town Mill Lane.

Longs Court Jesse Long (1853–1923) came to Whitchurch from West Meon in 1881 and set up as a grocer in a shop in the Market Place. The thatched-roof building caught fire and burnt down in 1895 and as he also sold gunpowder the spectacle must have been dramatic. The premises were rebuilt by the following year and were subsequently occupied by Samuel Bennett, International Stores, Gateway, Somerfield and more recently by the Co-op. In 1909 the adjoining ironmongery business was managed for Bennett by Cecil Ernest Duddington (1880–1953) and then leased to him in 1919. Cecil's sons Cecil, Horace and Ernest later ran the business – a veritable Aladdin's cave. (See **Bicester Close**.)

Long made jam in a factory he built in Bell Street where Longs Court is now and also manufactured mineral water, fruit squash, canned fruit and boiled sweets together with cider in a building where Hartley Meadow is situated. As Bell Street was too narrow for lorries to load, a new access was made for them in Church Street which is now incorporated into the entrance to Longs Court. Long's became a limited company in 1910 and production was at a peak between the two world wars. Jesse passed the business to his son George, but he became insolvent and in 1950 it was sold to T G Tickler, jam manufacturers of Grimsby, who traded under the name of Crosbie's Pure Food Company Ltd. From 1961 the buildings were used by several warehousing companies and then the plot was sold to a housing association in 1997.

Also on the site were Jesse Long's Plymouth Brethren meeting room and the Whitchurch Gas Company, which opened in 1856 and at first supplied gas for 21 street lamps in the town. From September to March lamps were lit from one hour after sunset to one hour

Whitchurch Street Names

London Street

The White Hart Hotel on the left has cellars dated 1500. It was known as a hostelry in c. 1619 and although considerably altered over the years the present building dates back to c. 1700. Beyond is the Victorian White Hart tap where coachmen lodged while their passengers stayed in the hotel. This was demolished to make way for a car park. Rolls of fabric displayed on the right are outside Harry Nash's drapery shop. He later moved into Newbury Street (see page 20). Further along is John Roe's Brewery House.

London Street

The Red House, built in c. 1525, was an inn from c. 1730 and faced with red brick in 1770 from which it takes its name. Further on is the inclined path known as Lynch Hill. A chalk escarpment caused by workings of the whiting factory can be seen in the distance.

before sunrise, but not on the seven nights in each lunar month when there was a full moon. The works were demolished in 1959.

Lord Denning Court Born above his parents' drapery shop in Newbury Street in 1899, Alfred Thompson Denning was the fifth of six children and attended the National School in Fairclose. He later joined other Whitchurch children taken on the train to the grammar school in Andover founded by John Hanson. Tom Denning took his first degree in mathematics at Magdalen College, Oxford but then turned to jurisprudence. He was appointed a High Court judge in 1944 and president of the National Marriage Council in 1949. Created Baron Denning of Whitchurch in 1957 he was appointed a Lord of Appeal in the same year. Then he became Master of the Rolls in 1962, an appointment held for 20 years. Lord Denning returned to Whitchurch in 1963 to live at The Lawn close to the fifteenth-century cottage where his parents had spent their retirement. He died in 2000. Lord Denning Court is on the site previously occupied by John Hide's first drapery shop (1866), later Harwood's grocery and bakery business and then offices of Kingsclere & Whitchurch Rural District Council.

Lower Evingar Road was the site of Edwin Fear's cattle market close to the Great Western Railway station and in the early twentieth century was known as Rampton's Field. James Hide purchased part of it from Charles Rampton in 1933 and in the following year built pairs of houses on both sides of the thoroughfare. The road was unmade and gated both at Bell Street and also at the Evingar Road end. A short rough track led north to Evingar Road and this became a lane in the late 1940s, giving vehicular access to Evingar Road. When it was widened in 1969 to provide a through road for traffic the owners of the house and bungalows built on the western side by Boast Bros. relinquished part of their front gardens. Also **Evingar Gardens**. (See **Pesthouse Lane, Stares Lane**.)

The Lynch In ancient field systems lynchets form on the downside of sloping fields that are repeatedly ploughed, so creating a bank, terrace or ledge of soil at the lower side. The word 'lynch' is used mostly in Hampshire and Dorset. However it is not clear how this is relevant to Whitchurch as the name was originally given to the area where many cottages had been built on the south-east-facing slope on the north side of London Street. Their gardens extended down to the river Test but were separated from the dwellings by a narrow lane, currently called The Lynch. This extends for about 150m before rejoining London Street and was probably part of the original road before it was realigned in *c.* 1750 to its present position closer to the river.

Whitchurch Street Names

Lynch Hill is an inclined path that leads up from London Street through The Lynch and then continues as a footpath running above the chalk escarpment, resulting from excavations by the whiting factory, and ending on the London Road near the Prince Regent public house. This factory was started before 1860 by Henry Rogers in a chalkpit to provide domestic material for whitening. It continued until Joseph Webb demolished it in 1896 and had pairs of houses built on the site, appropriately called Highcliff. The Lynch has also been used as a name for the path known as **Chatter Lane**.

The sloping east-facing strip of land to the east of houses in Lynch Hill Park, now covered with scrub and trees, is shown on an 1839 map as Mayors Lynch, with Winterton Bottom the pasture going down to the bed of the intermittent stream or winterbourne which flows into the Test at Bere Mill. The Lynch in Overton was considered unsuitable for agriculture and described as 'waste', and Southington Mill stands on the site of the thirteenth-century Lynch Mill.

Lynch Hill Park Close to The Lynch and with houses erected in a parkland setting in grounds attached to Berehill House, the name was suggested by the first residents in 1970.

McFauld Way Kathleen McFauld (1916–71) was active in the social and political affairs of the town and was a strong supporter for retaining the Church Hall (now Parish Hall) for secular activities when the Church had ideas of selling it because of the cost of its maintenance. Kath was manager of the Co-operative shop in Newbury Street, sometime chairman of the Parish Council and prominent in the British Red Cross Society in Whitchurch.

Mann Close Invariably opening a conversation with a witty quip, Orson Kennedy Mann (1904–75, but always O K Mann) was a builder and undertaker in London Street. He was a town councillor and chairman of the Scouts Committee.

Mansell Court A development in Station Road that was previously an industrial site. The name suggested by Whitchurch Town Council was to commemorate Richard Lloyd Maunsell (1868–1944), chief mechanical engineer for the Southern Railway 1923–37. His engine designs included the King Arthur, Lord Nelson and Schools classes. Although the name Maunsell was submitted to the Borough Council it was confirmed as Mansell.

Market Place (also known as **The Square)** A market hall or guildhall stood at the intersection of the five roads of the town. This was demolished sometime after 1796. Until the A34 bypass was built in

Origins of Whitchurch Street Names

1976, the Market Place had been busy with heavy traffic from the Midlands coming through Whitchurch on its way south to the coast and Southampton docks. Also in the eighteenth century a building of *c.* 1450 probably with a civic function, currently called The Beehive, had its eastern end truncated to widen access through the Market Place.

It had also been busy in earlier times. The Salvation Army Corps was formed in Whitchurch in 1881 only three years after William Booth had renamed the East London Christian Revival Union Mission as the Salvation Army and based it on a military pattern. The first citadel in Whitchurch was situated in Mrs Chappell's Silk Mill (The Factory) in Winchester Street. However opposition to Salvationists began here soon after the Army started, mostly because some inhabitants were upset by their marching and parading through the streets and in The Square, and because of their doctrine of temperance. Such unrest went on for several years and in 1889 Salvationists were arrested and marched to Winchester gaol. A 'Great Demonstration for Liberty' was held in October 1889 when more than 2,000 Salvationists gathered in The Square to listen to speeches by Commissioner Eva Booth and her son Commandant Herbert Booth. Representatives of the Army were summoned to appear at Winchester County Assizes but they

Market Place
A market hall that stood at the intersection of the five roads was demolished in the late eighteenth century. The building on the left, now known as The Beehive, was built in c. 1480 and probably had a civic function. The right-hand end was later demolished to widen access through the Market Place. The Kingsley Temperance Hotel, built in about 1911, replaced a building that housed the Whitchurch Post Office.

appealed to have their case heard in the High Court. The defendants pleaded guilty to obstruction and disturbance and the Lord Chief Justice, Lord Coleridge, told the jury that 'unless they had been satisfied that there had been a real and substantial nuisance they must acquit the defendants'. The verdict was Not Guilty. As Lord Denning wrote in 1990, 'One hundred years ago history was made in our little town of Whitchurch. We established the right of citizens to demonstrate and go in procession, so long as it is done peaceably and in good order. It was a famous Victory for Liberty in England.'

During this time there were other disturbances here. A General Election was called in 1885 following Gladstone's Third Reform Act of 1884 which enfranchised agricultural labourers. Voting took place on 30 November in the Andover divisional seat that included Whitchurch and during the afternoon a crowd assembled in Market Place. Then after dusk a mob of 300–400 became unruly and attacked the Conservative Party's headquarters and also locked the only two policemen on duty that night inside their police station. They then broke most of the windows in the Town Hall, smashed the front door and windows of the White Hart Hotel and attempted to take possession of the ballot box. Most of the ringleaders of the mob were known locally, but at a special session set up in Kingsclere in January 1886 no felonious intentions were proved although a few of the activists did receive fines for criminal damage. (See **Town Hall Court**.)

Meadow View An area backing onto fields that was earlier used by Warwick & Barr's haulage business. (See **Warwick Close**.)

Micheldever Road Up to at least the First World War this was known as Knowle Lane because almost 2km from its junction with Winchester Road it passes a wood known as Knowle Hassock and also Knowle Clump, a group of trees on a high point (124m) from where one was said to be able to see Southampton Water. It was first renamed Micheldever Station Road and later shortened to its current name.

Mulberry Mead Built in The Waterloo on the site of the workhouse, it is assumed that the name was used as a link with the silk industry in Whitchurch. Leaves of the White Mulberry tree provide the main food for silkworm larvae. However, silk was thrown, wound, warped and woven not only in the Silk Mill but also in several other buildings in the town. (See **Waterloo Court**.)

Neuvic Way In the 1970s Testbourne School forged a link with a school in Neuvic, France, chosen because it was of similar size and with the same types of industry as Whitchurch. In 1980 a Twinning

Origins of Whitchurch Street Names

Association was formed and now in alternate years groups of adults exchange visits between towns, and close friendships have developed over 30 years.

Newbury Street *Bynstret* could have been the original name for Newbury Street but from 1730 had become Bearhill, Bere Hill, Bare Hill, Boar Hill or Berehill. It is possible that this name derived from a coarse grain called bere (or bigg) which from the eighteenth century was the hardiest of all barleys and was grown on poor land, especially in Scotland, to provide early feed for sheep. Brewers considered it inferior to other types for malting. Alternatively, the name could be Old English in origin and derived from *baer*, a swine pasture, or *bearu*, a grove. By 1881 the road was known as Newbury Street, and currently that part north of the junction with Oakland Road is called Newbury Road. It has its own house numbering in contrast to London Street/Road and Winchester Street/Road. From 1915 Berehill House, previously the home of Spencer Portal, housed an auxiliary home hospital with 40 beds for servicemen injured during the First World War.

Oakland Road In the eighteenth century this was called Hebrews Lane following a visit by John Wesley to Whitchurch on 26 September 1742 when in a field subsequently called Hebrews Meadow he preached on a text from St Paul's Epistle to the Hebrews. Sometime later it became Oakland Terrace from the group of sixteen houses built on the south side by Joseph Webb in the late 1800s. At first it was a cul-de-sac with pedestrian access over a stile onto Evingar Road, and one assumes that there were oak trees in the vicinity to suggest the name. Certainly an early photograph shows a fine old oak tree standing close by the Evingar Road end.

The Old School The National School together with the master's house in Fairclose were built in 1845 at a cost of £1,000. At first the school was attended by 150 children but was enlarged in 1892 to accommodate 340 pupils and again in 1897 for 400 pupils. It closed in 1973 and the children were moved to a newly built school near Town Mill. The building was used as an ambulance station from 1975 to 1986 but then became derelict and in 1994 was sold by the vicars of Whitchurch and St Mary Bourne with the sale proceeds given to the new school. It was converted into private residences in 2007.

Orchard Place In 1875 John Hide built a Particular Baptist Chapel for his family together with the family of Stephen Barnett, a farmer who lived at The Hop Garden, later called Fourfarthings, on the southernmost part of his garden and orchard attached to his drapery shop. It had seating for 100 people. The chapel closed in 1949

Whitchurch Street Names

Newbury Street
The White Hart Hotel is on the right and opposite are the five display windows of Charles Denning's drapery shop, the birthplace of Lord Denning. The three-storey Belgrave House, home of the physician and surgeon Edward Burgess, can be seen in the background.

Newbury Street
This picture looks towards the town centre with the garden wall of Berehill House on the left. The lower entrance gates to the estate are next to the Builders Arms, a beer-house built c. 1840 and demolished in the 1960s.

Origins of Whitchurch Street Names

and was then used as headquarters of Hants 178 Detachment of the British Red Cross Society and subsequently by various enterprises. Apartments were built on remains of the garden in the 1980s.

Pages Yard A forge belonging to the blacksmith Henry Page (1863–1928) stood by Little Town Bridge on the site now occupied by Blacksmiths Bridge House. From at least 1901, and while he was there, the area behind with cottages was known as Pages Yard. Subsequent blacksmiths included Walter Holloway and Frank Angel.

Park View An estate of houses built in 2009 off Wells Lane and straddling part of the defunct GWR railway line has views across to Hurstbourne Park. First laid out by the monks of St Swithun's Priory in Winchester in AD 802, parts of the Park were later remodelled in the eighteenth-century landscape style of Lancelot 'Capability' Brown. The author Charles Kingsley considered it to be the finest park in the South of England – perhaps after he had been entertained by its owner, the Earl of Portsmouth.

Pegasus Court Pegasus was the mythological winged horse that threw its rider Bellerophon and continued on its flight to heaven where it became a constellation. Thus far it has not been possible to determine how this street name is relevant to Whitchurch. Perhaps like Ardglen it was chosen 'out of a hat'.

Pesthouse Lane Currently this is a short lane extending north from Evingar Road which led past the site of the Whitchurch pesthouse. During the 1600s pesthouses were built well away from other dwellings to house local inhabitants and travellers who were suffering from the plague. The Whitchurch Burial Registers 1605–1837 record that 13 people died of the plague here in 1625. However, as this pesthouse was reputedly built in 1790 by Dutch or French prisoners of war and the last outbreak of the plague in England occurred in the mid 1600s, it is likely that its purpose was to accommodate those suffering from smallpox. Burial registers show that in the years 1745–1833 there were more than 60 deaths attributed to smallpox and fever in Whitchurch and 12 occurred in 1800. By at least 1841 the building had been converted into two cottages and in 1903 Jonathan Dance of Bere Hill Farm purchased the property as accommodation for farm employees. His son Edward demolished it and in 1969 built a bungalow which he called The Furrow on the site, incorporating a stone reclaimed from the old building engraved 'F J M 1790' into his new one.

In the nineteenth century Pesthouse Lane was the track or thoroughfare down which unfortunate people were taken on their last journey from the pesthouse to the churchyard at All Saints (All Hallows).

Whitchurch Street Names

This lane commenced where the current Pesthouse Lane is situated and where the railway station was built in later years and then down what was to become Evingar Road and Lower Evingar Road. The journey continued across Wood Street (Bell Street) and along Love (Wells) Lane, so avoiding the town centre. (See **Stares Lane**.)

Pound Meadow Village pounds survived until the end of the medieval system of communal farming and were areas bounded by a wall, fence or hedge to contain livestock from the common field. In Whitchurch a cow common was situated close by on the London Road. The present Pound Meadow is built on the site of the Long family's tennis court, previously known as The Swamp. This perhaps gives credence to the idea that **The Green** (q.v.) was used for livestock. Also **Pound View**.

Queens Road Opened in 1952 and named to commemorate the coronation of Queen Elizabeth II.

Rampton Road Henry Rampton (1922–2005) was a long-serving parish clerk to Kingsclere & Whitchurch Rural District Council. Both he and his brothers Peter, Sidney and Charles were keen sportsmen and prominent members of the town's cricket and football teams.

Richard Walker Court Richard Hillier Walker (1916–93) was the son of a medical doctor who worked in London, Kenya and Frome, Somerset. He attended Kings School, Bruton and then went on to St Thomas's Hospital, London for medical training. Whilst there he joined the London Youth Orchestra as clarinettist and was also an accomplished dancer in tango competitions. At the start of the Second World War Dr Walker joined the Royal Army Medical Corps in Algiers and Rome and arrived in Whitchurch in 1948, living with his family at The Vinery in Newbury Street next door to his surgery. They later moved to Tufton Manor. During 30 years here as a well-loved, respected and compassionate family doctor he also gave medical training to members of the British Red Cross Society, St John Ambulance Brigade and Police.

Riverside This short footpath leads off London Street towards the river Test with three houses built in the 1870s on the site of a silk-weaving shed.

The Rookery Rooks are colonial birds and here they nest at the top of tall sycamore trees. Residents will confirm that they continually communicate with each other using a noisy, coarse 'caw', and after foraging in fields the 'parliament' passes over the town on summer

Origins of Whitchurch Street Names

evenings as they return to their nests. The entrance to The Rookery was once the lower entrance to Berehill House. It had ornate gates and a small lodge and was next to the Builders Arms, a hostelry that was demolished in the 1960s.

Seeviours Court Tom Seeviour (1865–1926), builder and wheelwright, came from Dorset to Whitchurch in the late 1890s with his brother Arthur (1873–1915), a blacksmith. They set up a business here as builders, coachbuilders, plumbers and undertakers on this site close to Whitchurch gasworks. (See **Longs Court**.)

Sheppard Close George Sheppard (1905–90) worked in the water supply industry both at home and abroad and came with his wife Peggy to live at Red Leaf Cottage on his retirement in 1964. Their garden close to the river Test was often opened to the public. Soon both were involved in parish life and George became sidesman and member of the Parochial Church Council at All Hallows. In 1970 he was elected Vicar's Warden and successfully organized an appeal to raise money to repair and re-shingle the church spire that had been erected in 1887/8. George and Peggy left Whitchurch in 1976 for a second retirement in Derbyshire.

Skylark Rise (see **Lapwing Rise**)

Station Road The London & South Western Railway station was opened in 1854 and early census returns list the Station Cottages. However, it was only in the early 1900s that it was called Station Road.

Stares Lane An obsolete name. In the seven decennial census returns for Whitchurch 1841–1901 the town was divided into four areas or enumeration districts. Each of these was delineated by boundaries, usually streets of the town, and the names of occupants within each were recorded. In the five returns for 1841–81 Stares Lane appears as a boundary, for example '…on the North by a field called Land for Land, thence down Stares Lane and Blowswood Lane to the Harroway'. This junction, now called Dirty Corner, was an area where night-soil was deposited before Whitchurch had mains drainage. In 1841 Thomas Stares aged 30 is listed as a farmer in Wood (Bell) Street, and then in the 1851 Census the address of the two cottages that had been converted from the Pesthouse was given as 'Pest House, Stares Lane'. In 1901 one of the census enumeration districts comprised 'the North side of Bell Street commencing at Stares Farm, the whole of Newbury Street, Old Pest House…'. Consequently it would seem that the thoroughfare began as a farm lane with the name originating from the farmer who was here in the 1840s and the name was contemporaneous with Pesthouse Lane (now Evingar Road and Lower Evingar Road). The group of houses and barns close to the corner of Bell Street and Lower Evingar Road are still known as Stares Farm, to which Charles and Elizabeth Rampton came in the early 1920s with land extending up to Oakland Road. The whereabouts of the field Land for Land has yet to be determined. (See **Pesthouse Lane**, **Lower Evingar Road**.)

Testbourne Court Depending on the season the Bourne rivulet arises from various springs in the chalk in the environs of Stoke and St Mary Bourne. After about three miles it empties into the river Test and nearby was a mansion appropriately named Testbourne, previously known as The Heronry. This was destroyed by fire in December 1933 and the duc de La Trémoille, a prominent cavalry officer in the French army, lost his life. Also the Hon. James Rodney died from his injuries after he jumped from the blazing building. The mansion was rebuilt, but this was demolished and another one built in 2008.

It was to this area that the opera singer Harry Plunket Greene (1865–1936) came annually from 1902 to fish the brown trout. He related his fishing exploits in a book, again aptly entitled *Where the Bright Waters Meet*, first published in 1924 (revised third edition 1999). His favourite spot was close to the 'Beehive bridge on the Whitchurch Road'. However by 1924 he believed that tarring the road resulted in the fish turning black and so suggested to 'the authorities' that 'the dressing be withdrawn from the roads for a good half mile on either side of the village' (Hurstbourne Priors) and 'a primitive watering cart would lay the dust at far less cost than they could lay the tar'. Plunket Greene became vice-president of Whitchurch United Football Club in 1903.

Test Mews Originally this was a continuation of the path known as The Waterloo close to the river Test. The name Test, already in use in the early 1400s, is considered to be related to the obsolete Welsh *tres* – 'tumult, commotion, contention, uproar', although perhaps this is more applicable to the lower reaches than to our peaceful river. The farmer, radical and social reformer William Cobbett (1763–1835) ridiculed this river: by driving the first paper mill at Bere Mill to produce paper money, it changed 'all our properties, all our laws, all our manners, all our minds'. (See **Waterloo Court**.)

Test Road Frederick Weeks, a prominent Whitchurch builder, bought the plot called Factory Meadow or Pigeon House Meadow in 1901. Four years later he sold part of it to James Hide, a silk manufacturer who built a terrace of 14 houses. Whereas access to London Street had

Origins of Whitchurch Street Names

Test Road
The terrace of houses was built in Pigeon House Meadow for James Hide in 1906 and called Hawthorne Villas.

previously been by a wooden footbridge over the river, this development necessitated that a road bridge be built. For a short while it was called New Road. The current allotment area on the south side was once the playing field of the Whitchurch Academy (Rosary School) in London Street, owned by Charles and Frances Geer.

Town Hall Court Dwellings built to the rear of the Town Hall that was erected for Lord Middleton in 1786/7 and leased from Squire Robert Rawlins of Bere Hill House by the freeholders of Whitchurch in 1842. The Town Hall has a tiled roof in contrast to the Silk Mill which is slated and was built in c. 1815 after the opening of the Basingstoke Canal which facilitated the transport of Welsh slate. On the ground floor the Town Hall housed a reading room and the Mechanics' Institute, first opened in 1855, and then the local fire engine from 1923 until 1958 when a new fire station was built in Church Street.

Town Mill Lane leads to the site of a mill mentioned in the Domesday Survey of 1086. For many years the mill was known as Lloyds Mill. Henry Lloyd (1837–1919) had been miller from the 1860s and the business was taken on by his son Henry Llewellyn Lloyd (1869–1953) and milling continued here up until about 1949. More recently it was the home of Rosemary and Ron Eastman who studied the natural history of the kingfisher found on the river Test. (See **Kingfisher Close**.)

25

Whitchurch Street Names

Tufton Originally placed in the Hundred of Wherwell, Tufton or Tuckington was transferred to Evingar Hundred between 1831 and 1841. In the eleventh century it was known as Tochiton, a Saxon name for Tucca's farm, and in later centuries Thokeston, Tokinton and Tokyngton. Tufton manor was linked to the manor of Wherwell until 1698 when it was sold to Alice Wallop, mother of the first Earl of Portsmouth.

Warwick Close Leonard John (Jack) Warwick (1897–1986) was a partner in the hauliers Warwick & Barr who were based in a yard off Bloswood Lane. (See **Meadow View**.)

Waterloo Court The Waterloo was until the late twentieth century the name of a passage and area that led off Winchester Street towards a building (The Waterloo) where Mulberry Mead stands, and then curved south by garden allotments to rejoin Winchester Street through a path now called **Test Mews**. The original building of four brick-built cottages was purchased by the Vestry in 1771 and, after building work, was opened in 1775 as the Parish and later the Union Workhouse which provided accommodation for upwards of 40 inmates. In addition, adjacent, single-storey, thatched and mud-built cottages were obtained in 1800 and adapted as a 'sack manufactory' for the inmates (see Roy Smith's model of Whitchurch as it was in 1839, held in the council chamber of the Town Hall). These were converted to dwellings in 1817 and continued in use for another century. Following the opening of a workhouse in Overton this one closed in 1836, was sold and made into domestic accommodation. The building was demolished in 1968. 'Waterloo' is not mentioned in the early parish records, but those of 1824 and 1833 do mention the accommodation of 'discharged Soldiers and Sailors' and their wives, so this gives weight to the idea that the name did originate from the battle which ended Napoleon's military career in 1815. Its current use as Waterloo Court, a nearby development on the site of John Roe's brewery house, presumably serves to retain the name. A new Union workhouse was built in Whitchurch in 1847/9 and became known as **The Gables**.

Webbs Farm Close The Webb family farmed at Charlcot for more than 100 years. Joseph (1841–1910) first rented the farm from St Cross in 1898 and then put his youngest son Horace (1873–1901) in as manager. Unfortunately Horace died after three years and another son Ross Wilmot (1869–1934) took over. He was succeeded by his son Sidney Joseph, a notable amateur boxer, and then by his son Ross Wyndham. It was a mixed farm with cereals, potatoes and a milking herd which supplied milk to Horne's Dairy. Ross was passionate about farming but also about vintage Bentley cars, and many fortunate brides were driven to All Hallows Church in luxury. Although the farm buildings were demolished in the mid 1970s when this close was created, Gill and Ross continued farming the land until he died in 1999. Gill was a town councillor and long-serving chairman of the Parish Hall committee.

The Weir A weir is variously described as a dam or a fence of stakes across a river to catch fish although how this was applicable to The Weir in Whitchurch is not clear. Here it is represented as a causeway built of local flints together with stone from the West Country across water meadows and giving access to Fulling Mill, built on the site of a mill mentioned in the Domesday Survey. However in Hampshire a tumbling bay is also known as a weir and traditionally this would control the supply of irrigation water into water meadows. One can be seen on the east bank a few metres upstream of Fulling Mill and is a brick wall or ledge that allows water to overflow to a lower level when the river is in spate. Also, in Hampshire the sluice gates used to control water flow are known as hatches.

Wells Lane By at least 1870 this had been called Love Lane and was a narrow lane continuing the thoroughfare from Pesthouse Lane down to the church. On 5 August 1873 an Act was passed setting up the Didcot, Newbury and Southampton Railway, later the Great Western Railway, to link Southampton with the Midlands. The station building was erected on a site called The Mound and the line opened to the public on 1 May 1882. Many trains carried military personnel down to Southampton docks during both world wars and also the injured passed through the town on their way north from Southampton. Access to the station for hauliers and carters from both Bell Street and Church Street was by a parallel, private gated lane called **Station Approach**. After the line was closed in 1964 the two lanes were combined as Wells Lane. So far it has not been possible to determine the origin of the name.

Wheeler Close Richard Wheeler (1909–87) was a founder member of Whitchurch Local History Society. Also a member of the Town Council from 1971 to 1983 he was elected to the Borough Council in 1976 which he served until his death. In 1974 Dick became town mayor, the first appointment after the local government reorganization that placed Whitchurch in the Borough of Basingstoke & Deane and entitled the town to restore the mayoralty. He was a recipient of Royal Maundy in 1979.

Winchester Street/Road Originally called Duck Street from its association with the river Test at Great Town Bridge and Little Town

Whitchurch Street Names

Winchester Street
Albert Weeks's newsagent and stationery shop is on the left, now called the Old Paper Shop. Opposite is the Pineapple, a beer-house built in *c.* 1840.

Winchester Street
Looking toward Great Town Bridge, Lloyd Cook's grocery and bakery shop is on the left and opposite is the butcher's shop of David and Elizabeth Filmore. Later this was the residence of the auctioneer Herbert Johnson whose auction mart stood behind the railings. This area is now a residents' car park.

Origins of Whitchurch Street Names

Bridge, it had been renamed Winchester Street by at least 1881. It was probably the latest of the main Whitchurch streets to be opened as this area south of the intersection of five roads had been a marshy area without burgage plots on the west side.

Up until 1950 Winchester Street commenced at the Market Place and ended at Great Town Bridge and then continued down to Tufton as Winchester Road. Each had its own sequential house numbering, surely much to the confusion of postmen. This problem was solved by adding 50 to the house numbers in Winchester Road to give continuous numbering along the thoroughfare. As noted above a similar situation occurred in London Street/Road in contrast to Newbury Street/Road.

Witan Court The name reflects the finding of ancient artefacts in the area during the preparations for building houses in 1998. The Witan was a predecessor of our parliament when Anglo-Saxon kings summoned bishops, thanes and aldermen to discuss religious, political, economic and foreign policies. (See **Caesars Way**.)

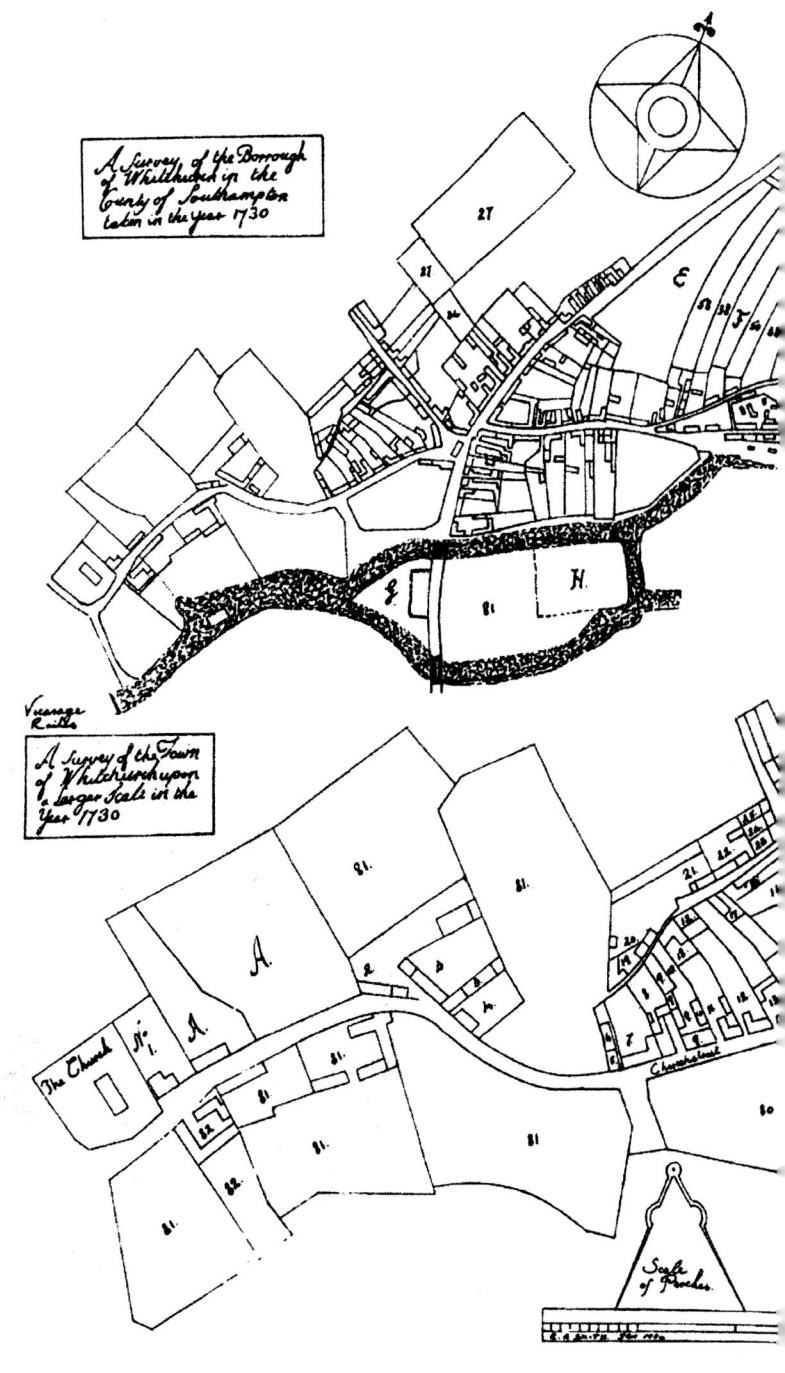

A Survey of the Borrough of Whitchurch in the County of Southampton taken in the year 1730

A Survey of the Town of Whitchurch upon a Larger Scale in the Year 1730

The Church

Scale of Perches

urch in 1730